ACTION KARATE

George R. Parulski, Jr.

 Sterling Publishing Co., Inc.   New York

*To my parents who
taught me to look,*

*And to my teachers who
taught me to see!*

EDITED BY LAUREL ORNITZ

Library of Congress Cataloging-in-Publication Data

Parulski, George R.
   Action karate.

   Includes index.
   Summary: Text and photographs introduce the
techniques of karate including stances, blocks,
punches, and kicks.
   1. Karate—Juvenile literature. [1. Karate]
I. Title.
GV1114.3.P365   1986   796.8'153   85-26257
ISBN 0-8069-6268-2
ISBN 0-8069-6269-0 (lib. bdg.)

Copyright © 1986 by George R. Parulski, Jr.
Published by Sterling Publishing Co., Inc.
Two Park Avenue, New York, N.Y. 10016
Distributed in Canada by Oak Tree Press Ltd.
% Canadian Manda Group, P.O. Box 920, Station U
Toronto, Ontario, Canada M8Z 5P9
Distributed in the United Kingdom by Blandford Press
Link House, West Street, Poole, Dorset BH15 1LL, England
Distributed in Australia by Capricorn Ltd.
P.O. Box 665, Lane Cove, NSW 2066
Manufactured in the United States of America

Contents

Introduction

The purpose of this book is to provide an introduction to the basic techniques of karate. The book is put together in a way that will make it easy for you to use for review or self-instruction.

I have studied and taught karate for more than 20 years. My first karate teacher, Frank Lane, was a pioneer of karate in America. He was one of the original students of the Japan Karate Association, which was started by the founder of Japanese karate, Gichin Funakoshi. Unlike other karate instructors, I have not changed the original karate program. I have kept it the same to preserve the purity and effectiveness of traditional Japanese karate, also known as *shotokan karate-do*.

Shotokan karate is an extremely effective system of self-defense that teaches powerful body movements started by strong actions of the hip. What makes the shotokan system stand out most from other forms of karate is the importance it places on throwing the whole body into the techniques. This way, even a small person can deliver an effective punch or kick.

I have taught many young people the art of karate. Not everything that works for an adult suits a young person. You need a special training program for your particular needs. And you need to be told why a technique works, in a way that is understandable to you. This book has been written with this in mind.

I truly hope that you will follow the book carefully, train hard, and gain skill in this great martial art. The end result will be self-discipline, self-control, and a better understanding of yourself.

Illus. 1. George R. Parulski, Jr.

1

The Meaning of Karate

No one knows for sure where karate-style fighting started. Some say it began almost 2,000 years ago in China. Others say the karate-like techniques of kicking, striking, throwing, and grappling began in India among the warriors.

In the year 520 A.D., an Indian monk named Bodhidharma travelled to China. When he got to the Shaolin monastery, he tried to teach the monks the workouts practised by the Indian warriors, but the workouts were too strenuous for the Chinese monks. So Bodhidharma taught them easier movements with breathing techniques from yoga, a system of exercises for developing control of mind and body.

The monks combined Bodhidharma's techniques with their own native fighting art. The new system that was born became known as *shaolin kung fu*. Kung fu caught on quickly in China. In 1372 some Chinese monks travelled east to the Pacific island of Okinawa and took kung fu with them.

The Okinawans had a fighting style of their own, called *tode*. When they learned kung fu, they combined it with tode techniques. The result was a new art called *Okinawan-te* (*te* means "hand").

Te grew more and more popular. By the early 1900s, it was taught in Okinawan public schools. One of the students who learned it, Gichin Funakoshi, went to Japan in 1922 and introduced te to the Japanese. He called the fighting style *kara-te*, which means "the empty hand." His style of karate was later called *shotokan*.

Funakoshi died in 1957 at the age of 88. To him, karate was not only a great fighting system, it was also a tool for building character. He wrote in his book *Karate: My Way of Life:*

> As a mirror's polished surface reflects whatever stands before it, and a quiet valley carries even small sounds, so must the student of karate render his mind empty of selfishness and wickedness in an effort to react appropriately towards anything he might encounter.

Karate is now taught for self-defense in karate schools (*dojos*) and police academies, and on army bases. Many colleges and universities teach it for credit in physical education. You can learn many different styles of karate. And you can do it whether you're male or female—no matter how young or old you are.

When you practise karate, you don't actually strike or kick your opponent. If you hit each other, you could seriously injure each other. Instead you control your movements so that you stop just short of making contact. The point of karate is to show that you could break through your opponent's defense and hit him or her if you had to. People who practise karate are called *karatekas*. Since karate is an art concerned with character as well as self-defense, karatekas are expected to show good sportsmanship and respect for their opponents.

There are two major types of karate competition:

point fighting and full-contact karate. In point fighting, you don't make contact with your opponent, but you wear protective gloves and footgear, just in case. You get a full point when you deliver a powerful kick, punch, or strike that would hit a vital area if it actually touched your opponent. In full-contact karate (also known as kick boxing), players wear boxing gloves and deliver kicks and punches at each other until one player is knocked out.

The Basic Principles

In karate, you learn how to punch (*tsuki*), strike (*uchi*), kick (*keri*), and block (*uke*). Punching, striking, and kicking are offensive techniques; blocking, on the other hand, is a defensive technique. These skills are the building blocks for the advanced techniques. You can easily learn the basic techniques in just a few months, but perfecting them takes a lifetime of daily practice. That's why it's so important to learn how to do them correctly from the start.

To learn shotokan karate, you need to study under a teacher who has been certified by a recognized Japanese martial arts organization. This way you can be sure you're learning the real thing.

Your performance in shotokan karate is judged by how well you've mastered skills in a few important areas:

Ability to Concentrate Power
In order to put the greatest power into a karate movement, you need to be able to concentrate strength from your entire body. You don't just punch with your arm or

kick with your leg. The power must come from the center of your body and then travel through your arm or leg into your hand or foot.

Concentration of power is called *kime* in Japanese, which means "focus" in English. To focus your technique, you need constant practice and training in the basic skills. You also need to learn how to relax your muscles at the start of a movement and tense them only just short of contact.

Speed and Power

In shotokan karate, power depends on speed and body size (mass). Muscular strength is not quite so important. Power is calculated by the equation:

P (power) = S (speed) × M (mass)

To get full power, you need to be able to use force from your entire body at the moment just short of impact. This force, however, is greatly affected by the weight of your punching arm (or kicking leg) and the speed at which your hand (or foot) is travelling. The punch of an advanced karateka can travel as fast as 43 feet per second. If the karateka weighs 100 pounds, he or she will deliver a generated force of 1,000 psi (pounds per square inch) on impact.

To get this kind of punching (or kicking) power, you need to perform the techniques in the traditional way, exactly as you were taught them. This is easy to do in practice, but very difficult to do in a dangerous situation or in a competition. You need to practice every day in order to develop the fast reflexes needed for making the right moves at the right times.

Rhythm and Timing

Rhythm is the ability to create the correct tempo for a karate movement. When your rhythm is just right, you:

Apply strength at the correct moment,
Control the speed from one technique to the next,
Make smooth transitions between movements.

Timing is very important. If your timing is off, your technique will not work. When your timing is right, you:

Start your defense in a way that will make your technique effective—if you are an expert, you'll be able to know by the way your opponent is standing or beginning a movement, the best position for starting a correctly timed defense,

Return to a stable position after performing your technique,

Stay relaxed and alert, with your body ready to launch your next movement.

The Role of Muscles

Many people believe that karate requires no muscular strength, but they are mistaken. Even if you have focus (*kime*), speed, timing, and rhythm, your techniques will not be strong if your muscles are weak. You don't need to build muscles (as in weight training), but you should tone and strengthen them by doing karate exercises and by constantly repeating the basic techniques.

Balance and Correct Form

Karate is an art that requires your best possible form and balance. In order to get the most out of your technique, you must do it in perfect form, being aware of the fine points that make the technique effective. You must be able to do a one-legged stance so that you can deliver a kicking technique or block attacks to your legs. For effective kicks and stable stances, you need a good sense of balance.

2

Stances

Your stance is right when you stand with good posture and stability. If your body is off balance, your techniques will not be effective. Stance in karate refers mainly to the lower portion of your body, especially your legs. You need to do all the punching and blocking from a strong, stable base.

Your stance is correct if:

It is well balanced so that you can do all the techniques with equal ease,

It allows freedom of movement—it should not be stiff,

It allows you to use the muscles that are needed for each movement.

You need to have a stance that is well balanced enough for performing blocking methods and strong enough for delivering punching techniques. There are hundreds of techniques in karate. It takes a lot of practice to be able to know which techniques will work best with the various stances. You need to be relaxed enough to be able to switch from one stance to the next, yet tense enough to keep yourself from being knocked over. When you are performing stances correctly, you are able to use the necessary muscles for effective punching, striking, and kicking. Incorrect stances result in weak techniques.

The main stances in shotokan karate are described in this chapter. Each stance is designed for a special purpose. Take enough time to master the basic stances, otherwise it will be impossible to do the advanced techniques.

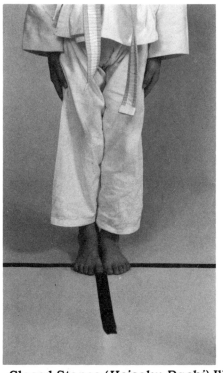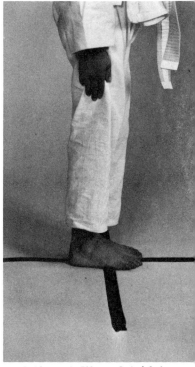

Closed Stance (*Heisoku-Dachi*) Illus. 2 (front), Illus. 3 (side). Place your feet together so that they touch each other. Keep your knees slightly bent and relaxed.

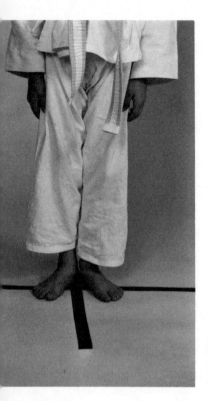

Open-Toed Stance (*Musubi-Dachi*) Illus. 4 (front), Illus. 5 (side). This is similar to the closed stance, except that you turn your toes outward at a 45° angle, keeping your heels together. This stance gives you a little more stability than the closed stance.

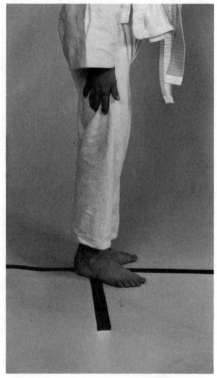

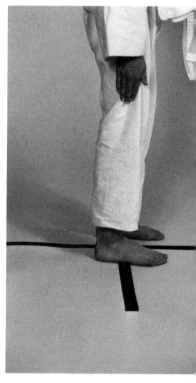

Open-Legged Stance (*Hachiji-Dachi*) Illus. 6 (front), Illus. 7 (side). This is a very natural and comfortable stance with many uses. Place your feet so that your heels are about 8 inches apart and your toes are turned outward.

Parallel Stance (*Heiko-Dachi*) Illus. 8 (front), Illus. 9 (side). This is performed exactly the same as the open-legged stance, except that your feet are parallel to each other.

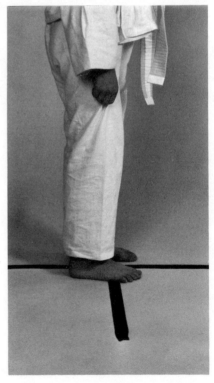

Inverted Open-Legged Stance (*Uchi-Hachiji-Dachi*) Illus. 10 (front), Illus. 11 (side). With this open-legged stance, you turn your toes inward.

T-Stance (*Teiji-Dachi*) Illus. 12 (front), Illus. 13 (side). In this stance, your feet form a "T", with the back foot (the top of the "T") turned slightly inward. About 12 inches should separate the heel of the front foot from the instep of the back foot.

Horse Stance (*Kiba-Dachi*) Illus. 14 (front), Illus. 15 (side). Position your feet at twice the width of your shoulders, bending your knees as if you were sitting on a horse. Keep your back straight and look straight ahead. Turn your feet inward and keep your hips low. You should flex your buttocks, but keep your ankles and knees relaxed. This stance is extremely stable from side to side.

Forward Stance (*Zen-Kutsu-Dachi*) Illus. 16 (front), Illus. 17 (side). Also known as the front stance, this is one of the most important stances in karate for both offensive and defensive techniques. It is stable from the front and rear, and somewhat stable from side to side. Keep a distance of 32 inches between your front and back feet, tensing your ankles for stability. Turn your front foot slightly inward, and turn your back foot towards the front as much as possible. Distribute your body weight 60 percent on your front foot and 40 percent on your back foot.

Back Stance (*Kokutsu-Dachi*) Illus. 18 (front), Illus. 19 (side). This stance is extremely stable from the rear and useful in blocking attacks to the front. It is best if you block a frontal attack in a back stance and then switch to a forward stance to deliver a counterattack. For the back stance, your feet should be about 32 inches apart. Tense the ankle of your rear foot, keeping the sole planted firmly on the ground. Place the heel of your front foot less firmly on the ground so that you can easily switch from stance to stance. Force the knee of your rear leg outward as much as possible, distributing your weight 65 percent on your rear leg and 35 percent on your front leg.

Straddle-Legged Stance (*Shiko-Dachi*) Illus. 20 (front), Illus. 21 (side). Also called the square stance, this is the same as the horse stance, except that you turn your feet outward at a 45° angle and you lower your hips closer to the ground.

Hourglass Stance (*Sanchin-Dachi*) Illus. 22 (front), Illus. 23 (side). Spread your feet the same width as your hips. Place the heel of your front foot on the same line as the big toe of your rear foot. Point the front foot inward at a 45° angle. The rear foot should point directly forward. Bend both knees inward slightly, and keep your leg muscles tensed. This stance is good for power techniques and is useful for both offensive and defensive movements.

Cat Stance (*Neko-Ashi-Dachi*) Illus. 24 (front), Illus. 25 (side). To perform this stance, start from a back stance and then slide your front foot back until your feet are about 12 inches apart. Position your front foot so that it rests on the ball. Distribute your weight 90 percent on your rear foot and 10 percent on your front foot.

One-Legged Stance (*Tsuri-Ashi-Dachi*) Illus. 26 (front), Illus. 27 (side). This stance is not very stable. It is only used in a few situations, such as before you deliver a kick or when you raise your leg to keep your opponent from striking it. Hook the instep of the lifted leg around the knee of the support leg. Bend the support knee, while slightly tensing your hips and ankles.

3

Punching Techniques

Punching techniques need to be delivered from a stable stance (see Chapter 2). To perform a powerful punch, you need to use your arm and shoulder muscles, as well as a jerking movement of your hips. The basic punching (*tsuki*) techniques in karate are described in this chapter.

Straight Punch (*Choku-Zuki*)

Important Points:
1. Keep your fist very tight. Strike just short of your target with only the knuckles of your index and middle fingers.
2. Stand up straight. Do not lean in any direction.
3. Punch in a straight line. Do not curve your punching movement.
4. Keep your shoulders relaxed and in a natural position. Do not raise one shoulder above the other or let one move ahead of the other.
5. Relax your entire body. Only tense your muscles just short of impact with your target.

Illus. 28 (top left). Begin the punch from an open-legged stance, with one fist extended.

Illus. 29 (top right). Thrust your fist at a target directly ahead. As you thrust, turn your forearm inward 180°.

Illus. 30 (right). Finish the punch with the back of your fist facing upwards and your arm extended as if you were thrusting a spear.

Reverse Punch (Gyaku-Zuki)

Important Points:

1. When thrusting your hips forward, keep them low and in a straight line with your opponent.
2. Keep the soles of your feet firmly planted on the ground.
3. Punch in a straight line towards your target. To make sure you do this, let your elbow brush your side as you deliver your punch.
4. Jerk your hips forward into the punching movement as fast as possible.
5. Do not lean forward into the punching movement. Keep your posture erect instead.

Illus. 31. Begin the punch from a forward stance, extending one arm over your front leg and holding your punching fist above your hip.

Illus. 32. As you punch, start to twist your hips forward while you turn your forearm inward 180°.

Illus. 33. Twist your hips completely forward as you straighten your back leg, extending your fist after a 180° turn. The forward-twisting movement of the hips gives this punch its power.

Illus. 34. Striking an opponent in the midsection with the reverse punch.

Lunge Punch (*Oi-Zuki*)

Note: The lunge punch is delivered after a long step forward, which causes a large shift in balance in your body. This forward boost gives a lot of power to your punch.

Important Points:
1. Step forward smoothly with your back leg. Make it light but fast.
2. Do not raise your back foot off the ground.
3. Punch with the thrusting power coming from your hip, not from just your arm and shoulder.

4. After your stepping-forward movement is completed, straighten your back leg when your fist is just short of contact.

Illus. 35. Begin this punch in the same starting stance you used for the reverse punch.

Illus. 36. Begin to step forward with your back leg, finally bringing it even with your front leg.

Illus. 37. As you begin to step forward, start twisting your forearm inward 180°. To increase your power, drive the stepping leg forward with a jerking movement of your hips.

Illus. 38. Finish the stepping-forward movement as you fully extend your punching arm.

Illus. 39. Two opponents face each other in fighting stances.

Illus. 40. As the boy on the left begins his punching action, the other boy begins to step forward.

Illus. 41. Before the boy on the left can complete his punch, the other boy steps completely forward and delivers a lunge punch.

Vertical Punch (Tate-Zuki)

Important Points:

1. Follow the same points given for the reverse punch, except do not twist your fist the full 180°.

2. Since the vertical punch is a fast technique, immediately return your fist back to your hip after completing the punch.

Illus. 42. Begin this punch in the same starting position you used for the reverse punch.

Illus. 43. Begin the punching action, twisting your forearm inward as you thrust your hips forward.

Illus. 44. Twist your fist only 90° (a quarter turn), striking just short of your target in a vertical position.

Illus. 45. A good target area for the vertical punch is the middle of the chest.

Illus. 46. The area under the chin is another good target area.

Close Punch (Ura-Zuki)

Important Points:

1. These points are the same as those for the reverse punch.
2. Flex the muscles of your back and side just short of contact, otherwise your punch will be weak.
3. The twisting action of the punch must be smooth and fast as you jerk your hips forward into the punch.

Illus. 47 (left). Start in a forward stance, with one hand extended and your punching fist held above your hip in a vertical position. **Illus. 48 (right).** Begin to twist your fist as you thrust your hips forward.

Illus. 49. The punch is completed with your hips thrust forward and your fist turned outward 90° (with the palm of your hand facing upwards).

Illus. 50. One opponent grabs the other around the neck in a choke hold.

Illus. 51. He steps forward towards his opponent.

Illus. 52. A close punch is delivered into his midsection. (Remember, in karate practice actual contact is not made.)

Hook Punch (Kagi-Zuki)

Important Points:

1. Your elbow should be kept bent at a 90° angle to your body.
2. Your punching fist should be about 6 inches from your chest.
3. To get the most power, step forward and to the side when you deliver this punch.
4. Your side muscles will naturally relax when you are delivering this punch, so be sure to flex them.

Illus. 53. Start in a back stance, with your punching fist above your hip.

Illus. 54. Begin the punch by twisting your fist 180° inward.

Illus. 55. Complete the movement by punching to the side, at a right angle to your target. Keep your elbow bent at a 90° angle.

Roundhouse Punch
(Mawashi-Zuki)

Important Points:

1. Let your elbow brush your side until the last possible moment when your fist moves forward.
2. Be sure to thrust your hips forward into the punching action.

Illus. 56 (left). Start in a forward stance, with your punching fist above your hip and your other hand extended. Illus. 57 (right). Begin the punch by twisting your fist 180° inward. At the same time, begin to thrust your hips forward.

Illus. 58. The punch is completed with a circular hooking action as you thrust your hips forward for extra power.

Illus. 59. The boy on the right grabs the other boy's wrist.

Illus. 60. He steps up into a forward stance as he begins his punching action.

Illus. 61. The defense is completed when he delivers the roundhouse punch to his opponent's head. (Again, remember that in practice, actual contact is never made and especially to the head.)

4

Striking Techniques

Striking techniques are different from punching techniques because you do them with a snap of your elbow and forearm. To deliver a good striking technique (called *uchi-waza*), snap your forearm out smoothly and rapidly, using your elbow as the center of movement. Keep your elbow relaxed and slightly bent so that you don't extend it too much.

When you are delivering a strike, keep your shoulder relaxed, with tension only in your striking hand. Snap your hand forward and then tense the muscles of your arm and shoulder just short of contact. After that, relax the shoulder and snap the striking hand back to its original position as fast as possible. This sudden return of the striking hand creates the snap.

Back-Fist Strike *(Uraken-Uchi)*

Important Points:
1. Avoid striking with your entire arm. Strike only with the back of your fist near the knuckles of your index and middle fingers.
2. Point your elbow at your target before striking.
3. Always keep your elbow slightly bent so that you won't extend it too much.

Illus. 62. Start in a horse stance, with your right fist held over your left hand at your left hip.

Illus. 63. With your elbow as the center, snap your forearm out to your right side in a 180° arc.

Illus. 64. The technique is completed when your right fist is extended to your right side.

Illus. 65. Snap your fist back by bending your elbow.

Illus. 66. The boy on the right faces his opponent in a ready stance.

Illus. 67. As the boy on the left steps forward to punch his opponent's head, he sinks into a horse stance.

Illus. 68. As the boy reaches the full extension of his punch, his opponent delivers a back-fist strike to his side.

Elbow Strikes (Empi-Uchi)

Method 1: Side-Elbow Strike

Important Points:
1. Keep the forearm of your striking elbow very close to your chest as you strike out to your side.
2. Always look in the direction of your strike.

Illus. 69 (left). Start in a horse stance, with your right fist near your left ear and your left fist near your right hip. Illus. 70 (right). Begin to bring your left fist to your left hip as you strike out with your right elbow towards your right side.

Illus. 71 (left). Your left fist is now at your left hip, and your right elbow is extended fully to your right side. Illus. 72 (right). A good target area is the opponent's side, as you block his attack from overhead.

Method 2: Back-Elbow Strike

Important Points:
1. Draw your elbow back very powerfully.
2. Be sure to keep your fist close to the side of your body when striking your target.

Illus. 73. Start in a left-forward stance, with your right hand extended.

Illus. 74 (top left). Look to the right rear, as you begin to bring your right elbow back.

Illus. 75 (top right). Drive your right hip and right elbow back, as you rotate your forearm outward 180°.

Illus. 76 (left). The attacker grabs his opponent from behind in a bear hug.

Illus. 77. The opponent steps forward with his left foot, bringing his attacker's arms upwards.

Illus. 78. The opponent delivers a powerful elbow strike just short of his attacker's chest.

Method 3: Rising-Elbow Strike

Important Points:
1. Keep your arm close to your side as you bring your elbow upwards.
2. Be sure to jerk your hip into the striking action.
3. Tighten the muscles in your buttocks as you thrust your hips into the strike.

Illus. 79 (left). Start in a left forward stance, with your right fist held above your hip and your left fist extended. Illus. 80 (right). Begin to bring your left fist to your left hip as you bring your right elbow forward and upwards in a half circle.

Illus. 81. Jerk your right hip into the striking movement as you complete the strong upwards thrust with your right elbow.

Illus. 82. The boy on the left grabs his opponent around the neck with a choke hold.

Illus. 83. The opponent steps towards his attacker.

Illus. 84. He delivers a rising-elbow strike just short of his opponent's chin.

Knife-Hand Strikes (*Shuto-Uchi*)

Method 1: From Inside Outward

Important Points:

1. Always rotate your hips in the opposite direction of your strike.
2. Be sure to snap your arm the way you would in a back-fist strike.

Illus. 85 (left). Start in a right forward stance, with your right hand below your left ear and your left hand extended. Illus. 86 (right). Bring your left hand closer to your left hip as you begin the striking action.

Illus. 87. Bring your left hand all the way to your left hip. Rotate your hips counterclockwise, forming a horse stance as you strike with your right hand.

Illus. 88. The opponents face each other in a ready, natural stance.

Illus. 89. As the boy on the left attacks with a lunge punch, the other boy ducks out of the way.

Illus. 90. After the boy on the left has completed his punching action, the other boy strikes him under his punching arm with a right knife hand.

Method 2: From Outside Inward

Important Points:
1. Be sure that your fingers are rigid and held close together. Keep your wrist firm to make sure you get a good snap.
2. Remember to jerk your hip into the striking action.

Illus. 91 (left). Start in a left forward stance, with your left hand extended and your right hand held behind your right ear. Illus. 92 (right). Bring your left fist to your left hip as you begin to move your right hand with your right hip.

Illus. 93. Complete the hip rotation until your body faces forward as you snap the right knife hand with a 180° twist (the back of your hand should face the ground).

Illus. 94. A good target area for the strike is just short of the side of the head.

Hammer-Fist Strike *(Tettsui-Uchi)*

Important Points:
1. Be sure to make a snap by pulling your striking hand away from your target just short of impact.
2. Step into the striking action so that you add your body weight to the strike.

Illus. 95 (left). Start in a ready open stance. Illus. 96 (right). Step forward with your right leg as you raise your right fist above your head.

Illus. 97. Sink into a horse stance as you bring down your right hammer fist.

Illus. 98. The boy on the left grabs his opponent's left wrist.

Illus. 99. The opponent steps forward with his right foot into a horse stance as he pulls his seized left wrist towards his left hip.

Illus. 100. He delivers a smashing hammer-fist strike to his opponent's collarbone. (Of course, no contact is made in practice.)

5
Kicking Techniques

Many people are attracted to karate because of the kicking techniques. The kicks are beautiful and impressive to watch, and they have more power than attacks with the hands. The only drawback is that kicking techniques are very difficult to master. It takes a lot of practice before you can use them effectively.

To be able to deliver a good kick, you need correct form and good sense of balance. You need to begin your kick from a chamber position, which means bringing your foot to your knee before kicking. Then you need to finish your kick in that same chamber position. The better your chamber, the better and more effective your kick will be.

Front Kick (Mae-Geri)

Important Points:
1. Keep your support leg slightly bent when you deliver the kick.
2. Do not lean back as you kick. Try to lean into the kicking action.

3. Do not stand up on the ball of your support foot. This foot should be firmly planted on the ground.
4. Be sure to curl the toes back on your kicking foot to create a good surface for your kick.

Illus. 101. Start in a left forward stance, placing your hands near your face in a guard position.

Illus. 102. Keeping your left (support) leg planted firmly on the ground (the entire sole of your foot must remain on the ground), thrust your right hip forward as you raise your right leg so that your right foot is next to your left knee. This is the chamber position.

Illus. 103 (top left). Snap your right foot forward in a straight line to your target and then strike just short of your target with the ball of your foot.

Illus. 104 (top right). After kicking, immediately return to the chamber position.

Illus. 105 (right). Bring your kicking leg back, and return to a left forward stance.

Illus. 106 (top left). The boy on the right grasps his opponent's hands.

Illus. 107 (top right). The opponent chambers his kicking leg (the right one, in this case) and pulls the other boy towards him.

Illus. 108 (left). The opponent delivers a front kick to the other boy's midsection.

Side Kick (Yoko-Geri)

Important Points:

1. When kicking, be sure to lock your knee joint for a moment. This will add a lot of power to your kick.
2. The side kick works best when the edge of your kicking foot strikes your opponent at a 90° angle.
3. Be sure to keep your support leg slightly bent.
4. Lean into the kicking action, not away from it.

Illus. 109. Start in a ready open stance, with your head turned to the side.

Illus. 110. Shift your weight to your left leg and chamber your right foot to your left knee.

Illus. 111 (left). Kick to the side, locking your knee joint for a second, and then strike just short of your target with the edge of your foot. Illus. 112 (right). After the kick, return your foot to the chamber position.

Illus. 113 (left). Return to a ready stance. Illus. 114 (right). The boy on the left grabs his opponent's arm with both of his hands.

Illus. 115. His opponent pulls him closer as he chambers his kicking leg.

Illus. 116. The opponent delivers a side kick to the other boy's midsection.

Roundhouse Kick (*Mawashi-Geri*)

Important Points:

1. Do not just kick with your leg. You need to throw your hips into the kick by rotating them.
2. Be sure to snap your kicking leg back to the chamber position after you hit just short of your target. This snapping action adds great power to the kick.
3. When you twist your hips into the kick, your support leg will rotate slightly also. But be sure to keep the sole of your foot firmly planted on the ground. Do not raise up on the ball of your foot.

Illus. 117 (left). Start in a left forward stance, with your fists in a ready position. Illus. 118 (right). Raise your right knee upwards and to the side so that your right foot, lower leg, and knee are parallel to the ground at the level of your left knee. This is the chamber position.

Illus. 119 (top left). Rotate your hips counterclockwise and snap your right foot forward in a circle to the front of your body. Strike just short of your target with the ball of your foot or your instep.

Illus. 120 (top right). Return to the chamber position.

Illus. 121 (right). Place your kicking foot back on the ground behind you.

Illus. 122 (top left). The attacker faces his opponent with a club.

Illus. 123 (top right). As the attacker raises the club over his head, his opponent chambers his kicking leg.

Illus. 124 (left). He delivers a roundhouse kick to his attacker's groin before his attacker can strike him with the club.

Back Kick (*Ushiro-Geri*)

Important Points:

1. Aim your hip at your target to increase the power in your kick.
2. Kick directly back, as if you were a mule.
3. When striking your target, tighten your buttocks muscles to increase the force of your kick.

Illus. 125. Start in a ready open stance.

Illus. 126. Shift your weight to your left foot as you raise your right foot to your left knee (the chamber position).

Illus. 127 (top). Lean your body slightly forward as you thrust your leg directly behind you at your target. Strike just short of your target with your heel as you glance behind you to be sure you are hitting in the direction of your target.

Illus. 128 (left). Return to the chamber position.

Illus. 129 (right). Return to a ready stance.

Illus. 130 (bottom). The opponent grabs the other boy's wrists from behind.

Illus. 131. He steps forward as he chambers his kicking leg.

Illus. 132. He delivers a back kick towards his opponent's midsection.

6

Blocking Methods

Even if you have excellent punching, striking, and kicking techniques, they will be useless unless you also know how to block your opponent's attacks. Blocking techniques are ways of moving your body to stop your opponent's attack that leave you in a good position for delivering a counterattack—that is, a punch, strike, or kick of your own.

Rising Block (Age-Uke)

Important Points:

1. Complete the block with your forearm about 4 inches above you head.
2. Keep your elbow bent at about a 90° angle as you raise it from your hip to your forehead.

Illus. 133. Start in a right forward stance, with your right hand held in a fist at your right hip and your left hand held open above your head.

Illus. 134. Jerk your right hip forward as you begin to raise your right arm and lower your left arm.

Illus. 135. Move your left fist to your hip as you raise your right arm above your head.

Illus. 136. This technique is excellent for blocking strikes to the head.

Outside/Inward Block (Soto-Uke)

Important Points:

1. Be sure to bend your blocking arm 90° at the elbow.
2. Your elbow should be about 4 inches from your body.
3. Tense your arm muscles just short of contact with your target.

Illus. 137 (left). Start in a right forward stance, with your hips and shoulders facing forward. Hold your right fist above your right shoulder and your left fist in front of your chest. Illus. 138 (right). Twist to your left as you bring your left fist towards your left hip.

Illus. 139. Bring your left fist above your left hip. Drive your right arm forward and inward as you block.

Illus. 140. This technique is excellent for blocking punches to the midsection.

Inside/Outward Block (Uchi-Uke)

Important Points:

1. The main points are the same as those for the outside/inward block, except that the blocking action goes outward instead.
2. When shifting your weight to a back stance, be sure to twist your hip into the blocking movement.

Illus. 141 (left). Start in a ready open-legged stance. Illus. 142 (right). Step forward with your right leg into a right forward stance, crossing your arms in front of your chest.

Illus. 143 (right). Shift your weight to a left back stance as you bring your left fist above your left hip. Using your elbow as a pivot, rotate your right arm clockwise, and block from the inside outward.

Illus. 144 (bottom). This is an excellent technique for blocking attacks to your mid-section.

Low Block (Gedan-Barai)

Important Points:

1. Your blocking arm should rest about 6 inches above the knee of your forward leg.
2. To block powerful kicks, you need very strong blocking techniques. Be sure to block downwards with a lot of power in your arm and shoulder.

Illus. 145. Start in a ready open-legged stance.

Illus. 146. Step back with your left foot into a right forward stance. At the same time, bring your right fist under your left ear and extend your left fist downwards.

Illus. 147. Block downwards with your right forearm as you bring your left fist to your left hip.

Illus. 148. This is an excellent technique for blocking kicks to the groin.

Knife-Hand Block (*Shuto-Uchi*)

Important Points:

1. Do not bring your hand on your non-blocking arm to your side, as you do in other blocking techniques. Keep it at the middle of your chest instead.
2. Be sure to bend your blocking arm 90° at the elbow.
3. The key to this blocking method is the knife-hand formation. Used with enough force, this block can injure the arm or leg of your attacker.

Illus. 149 (left). Start in a ready open stance. Illus. 150 (right). Step back with your left foot into a left back stance. At the same time, with your hands in knife-hand formations (see Chapter 4), bring your right hand near your left ear with the palm facing your ear and extend your left hand forward with the palm facing the ground.

Illus. 151. Block forward with your right hand, turning it 180° so that you can strike just short of your target with the edge of your hand. At the same time, turn your left hand 180°, bringing it to the middle of your chest with your palm now facing upwards.

Illus. 152. This is an excellent technique for blocking attacks to the midsection.

Cross Block *(Juji-Uke)*

Important Points:

1. This is a very powerful block that a small person can use to block an attack from a larger, more powerful opponent.
2. Be sure to thrust your arm powerfully into the blocking action.
3. You can do this blocking technique downwards or above the head. And you can keep your hands in fists (as shown) or open in a knife-hand position.

Illus. 153 (left). Start in a ready open-legged stance. Illus. 154 (right). Step forward with your left leg into a left forward stance. At the same time, bring both fists above your hips.

Illus. 155. Cross one forearm over the other with a powerful thrusting action to create a blocking surface where the forearms meet.

Illus. 156. This is an excellent technique for blocking kicks to the groin area.

Illus. 157. The cross block can also be used for protecting yourself from overhead attacks with a club.

Wedging Block (*Kakiwake-Uke*)

Important Points:

1. For a more powerful block, be sure to use the boost you gained from sinking into a back stance.
2. Keep your elbows about 6 inches from your sides.

Illus. 158. Start in a ready open-legged stance.

Illus. 159. Step back with your right foot into a right back stance. At the same time, cross your arms in front of your chest with the inside of your wrists facing your chest.

Illus. 160. Twist your arms 180° so that the inside of your wrists face outward.

Illus. 161. The attacker grabs his opponent in a choke hold.

Illus. 162. The opponent steps into a back stance as he crosses his arms over his chest.

Illus. 163. He performs a wedging block to break the hold around his neck. Now he can use any counter-attack.

7

Falling Correctly

Breakfall techniques are special methods used for falling to the ground (or mat) that keep you from getting injured. Called *ukemi-waza* in Japanese, breakfall techniques are a major part of *judo* training. But it's also important for karate students to know how to protect their bodies as they hit the ground.

With any breakfall, you need to remember to:

1. Slap the mat (or ground) as hard as possible—this will reduce the shock of your fall,

2. Never fall on your spine—always protect the vital areas of your body,

3. Always keep your head tucked in to keep it from smashing on the ground.

Back Breakfalls *(Ura-Ukemi)*

Method 1

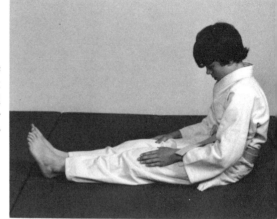

Illus. 164. Sit on the mat with your back curved, your head tucked in, and your hands resting on your knees.

Illus. 165. Roll back, keeping your head tucked, and get your hands ready to strike the mat.

Illus. 166. Strike the mat when the middle of your back touches the mat. Keep your head and your lower back off the mat.

Method 2: Leaping-Back Breakfall

Illus. 167. Squat on the mat with your head tucked in and your arms crossed in front of your chest.

Illus. 168. Leap into the air, pushing off with your legs.

Illus. 169. Fall to your back as you slap the mat. Be sure that your head and lower spine do not touch the mat.

Side Breakfalls (Yoko-Ukemi)

Method 1: Squatting

Illus. 170. Squat on the mat with your hands on your knees.

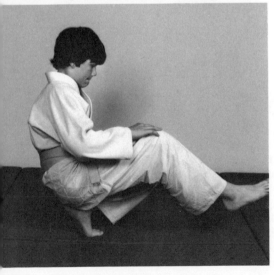

Illus. 171. Raise the foot on the side you are going to fall on (in this case, the right side) as you raise the hand on the same side.

Illus. 172. Fall to the side and slap the mat so that it takes in the shock of your fall.

Method 2: Standing

Illus. 173. Stand with your left foot ahead of your right foot.

Illus. 174 (left). Raise your right foot off the mat as you begin to lower yourself with your left leg. Get your right hand ready to slap the mat.

Illus. 175 (bottom). Fall to your right side and slap the mat to absorb the shock of your fall.

Front Breakfall (Zempo-Ukemi)

Illus. 176 (top left). Stand up straight with your hands raised in front of you.

Illus. 177 (top right). Begin to fall forward as you look to your side.

Illus. 178 (right). Strike the mat with your palms and forearms to keep your chest from hitting the mat.

Advanced Leaping Breakfalls (Zempo-Kaiten)

Method 1: To Side

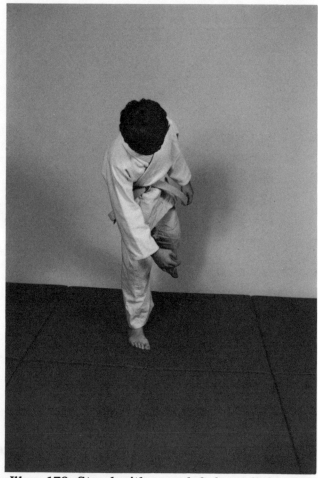

Illus. 179. Stand with your left foot off the mat as you face downwards.

Illus. 180. Leap into the air without using your hands for support.

Illus. 181. Fall to your left side, striking the mat with your left hand and your right foot.

Method 2: To Back

Illus. 182. Raise your left foot off the mat with your hands crossed in front of your chest.

Illus. 183. Leap into the air without letting your hands touch the mat.

Illus. 184. Fall to your back, slapping the mat with both hands and both heels. Be sure that your head and buttocks do not hit the mat.

8

Basic Combinations

Basic combinations are a series of techniques delivered in a particular order. They are blocks, punches, kicks, and strikes used against an imaginary opponent. To get the most out of the basic combinations, you need to put 100 percent of your effort and attention into them. Someone watching you should get the feeling that you are fighting a real opponent.

Here are some basic combinations. After you learn them, you should put your own combinations together. The way you combine your techniques shows your special style and personality.

Combination #1

Illus. 185. Start in a ready open stance.

Illus. 186. Step into a left forward stance and then deliver a rising block.

Illus. 187. Do a right reverse punch.

Illus. 188. Do a right front kick.

Illus. 189. Bring your kicking leg forward and deliver a right lunge punch.

Illus. 190. Finish the combination with a left reverse punch as you give a karate shout (*kiai!*) for extra power.

Combination #2

Illus. 191. Start in a ready open stance.

Illus. 192. Deliver a high right roundhouse kick.

Illus. 193. Turn counter-clockwise and deliver a left back kick.

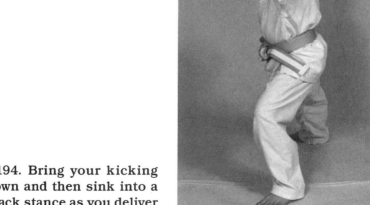

Illus. 194. Bring your kicking foot down and then sink into a right back stance as you deliver a left knife-hand strike.

Illus. 195. Shift your weight into a left forward stance as you deliver a right reverse punch. *Kiai* (shout)!

Combination #3

Illus. 196. Start in a ready open stance.

Illus. 197. Step into a left forward stance and then deliver a high cross block.

Illus. 198. Step forward into a horse stance and then deliver a right hammer-fist strike.

Illus. 199. Bring your feet together and look to the side as you chamber your leg.

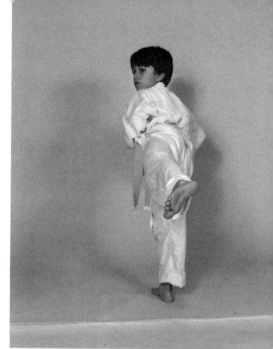

Illus. 200. Deliver a left back kick.

Illus. 201. Bring your kicking foot down and then deliver a left back-fist strike from a horse stance.

The Ranking System

In karate, you wear a colored belt around your waist that is tied in a square knot over your navel to signify your rank (official standing) or proficiency (how far you have advanced towards having a high degree of skill). In order to receive a belt, you are tested before a board of examiners who determines your score. Although passing grades vary from school to school, the average passing grade is a score of 75 percent.

The test includes a written and/or oral exam on the history and philosophy of karate, a demonstration of physical fitness, and a performance of karate techniques. The techniques are usually divided into four parts: basic techniques, formal exercise, self-defense skills, and free-fighting.

Several organizations award a special rank for children who are less than 10 years old. The belt has a white stripe down the middle or else just on the ends.

The colors of the belts approved by the All-Japan Seibukan Martial Arts and Ways Association stand for various ranks:

White = first-level beginner
Yellow = second-level beginner
Orange = third-level beginner
Green = first degree—first-level intermediate
Green = second degree—second-level intermediate

Brown = first degree—first-level expert
Brown = second degree—second-level expert
Brown = third degree—advanced student

These colored belts are considered low degree (*kyu*) and are numbered from eight to one in descending order. For example, when you get to the first low rank (*ik-kyu*), you wear a brown belt with three stripes. The three stripes stand for third degree. It takes about 3½ to 10 years to reach this rank, depending on how hard you work to perfect the techniques.

After the low-degree ranks come the graded (*dan*) ranks. At this stage, you wear a black belt. In shotokan karate, there are ten degrees of black belts, numbered in ascending order from one to ten. At the tenth level, you actually wear a red belt that signifies that you are a master.

In addition to graded ranks, the advanced student or teacher is granted titles. Everyone isn't awarded a title; only those with exceptional skill and determination receive this honor from Japan. These are the titles:

Expert (*Tashi*) Student wears a black belt with a ¼ inch white stripe down the middle.

Polished Expert (*Renshi*) Student wears a belt that is black on one side and white-and-red striped on the other.

Master (*Kyoshi*) Teacher wears a black belt trimmed in red.

Polished Master (*Hanshi*) Teacher wears a black-and-red blocked belt.

Superior Master (*Shihan*) Teacher wears a red belt.

About the Assistants

Illus. 202. Jason "Hot Shot" Hammersla is a student of both shotokan karate and judo, as well as a junior instructor at the author's school. Jason is also a member of the school's demonstration team, which competes at local and regional tournaments.

Illus. 203. Clayton "The Man" Tanner holds ranks in shotokan karate and judo. Clayton is a junior instructor at the author's school, where he also performs on the demo team.

Illus. 204. Jimmy "Hot Stuff" Ziegler is a student of both shotokan karate and judo, and is a member of the demo team at the author's school. Jimmy is especially determined and powerful for someone his size and age.

Illus. 205. Charlie "The Ninja" Parulski is a student of shotokan karate. Charlie is the author's son, and is on the demo team at his father's school. He is known for his punching ability and form, as well as his ability with ancient weapons. (*Ninja* is a Japanese word that refers to a martial arts master who uses ancient weapons and resembles a spy.)

Illus. 206. David "The Hurricane" Lomb is a student of judo and aiki-jujutsu at the author's school, where he also performs on the demo team. David has shown exceptional skill in competitions for someone his size and age.

About the Author

George R. Parulski, Jr. is known around the world as a writer and an authority on the techniques, history, and philosophy of the martial arts. Parulski is chief instructor of the Yama Ji: School of Traditional Martial Arts, located in Webster, New York. He has trained children as well as adults, and many of his adult students have been champions.

Parulski has the following degrees: fourth-degree black belt (*yondan*) in both shotokan karate and judo, fifth-degree black belt (*godan*) in judo, licensed teacher (*menkyo*) in the tenshin shin'yo-ryu style of aiki-jujutsu, third-degree black belt (*sandan*) in goju-ryu karate, first-degree black belt (*shodan*) in Japanese swordsmanship (*iai-do*), and a white sash in tai chi ch'uan kung fu and shaolin kung fu with emphasis on white crane movements.

He has written several other books on self-defense, as well as many articles for the leading martial arts magazines.

Parulski has two children, Jaclyn and Charles. He is the United States Representative for the All-Japan Seibukan Martial Arts and Ways Association and the Eastern Regional Director of Judo for the International Martial Arts Federation.

Glossary

Age-uke (ah-geh oo-kay) Rising block
Ate-waza (ah-teh wah-zah) Smashing techniques
Choku-zuki (cho-koo zoo-key) Straight punch
Chudan (chew-dahn) Midsection
Dojo (dough-joe) Training hall, or school
Empi-uchi (em-pee oo-chee) Elbow strike
Gedan (geh-dahn) Lower area of body
Gedan-barai (geh-dahn baa-rah-ee) Downwards block
Gi (ghee) Uniform
Gyaku-zuki (gya-koo zoo-key) Reverse punch
Hachiji-dachi (hah-chee-gee dah-chee) Open stance
Heiko-dachi (hay-koh dah-chee) Parallel stance
Heisoku-dachi (hay-sow-koo dah-chee) Closed stance
Hidari (he-dah-rhee) Left
Jiyu-kumite (gee-you koo-me-teh) Free-fighting or sparring
Jodan (joe-dahn) Head/face area
Juji-uke (jew-gee oo-kay) Cross block
Kagi-zuki (kah-gee zoo-key) Hook punch
Kakiwake-uke (kah-key-wah-kay oo-kay) Wedging block
Karate (kah-rah-teh) Empty-hand fighting
Kata (kah-tah) Formal exercises or karate dances
Keri-waza (kay-rhee wah-zah) Kicking techniques
Kiba-dachi (key-bah dah-chee) Horse stance
Ko-kutsu-dachi (koe-koo-tsu dah-chee) Back stance
Mae-geri (mah-eh geh-rhee) Front kick
Mawashi-geri (mah-wah-she geh-rhee) Roundhouse kick
Migi (me-ghee) Right
Musubi-dachi (moo-sue-be dah-chee) Open-toed stance
Neko-ashi-dachi (neh-koh ah-she dah-chee) Cat stance
Oi-zuki (oh-ee zoo-key) Lunge punch
Sanchin-dachi (san-chin dah-chee) Hourglass stance
Shiko-dachi (she-ko dah-chee) Straddle stance
Shuto-uchi (shoe-toe oo-chee) Knife-hand strike
Soto-uke (So-toh oo-kay) Outside/inward block
Tate-zuki (tah-teh zoo-key) Vertical punch
Teiji-dachi (teh-gee dah-chee) T-stance
Tsuki-waza (tsue-key wah-zah) Punching techniques
Uchi-uke (oo-chee oo-kay) Inside/outward block
Uchi-waza (oo-chee wah-zah) Blocking techniques
Uraken-uchi (oo-rah-ken oo-chee) Backhand strike
Ura-zuki (oo-rah zoo-key) Close punch
Ushiro-geri (oo-she-row geh-rhee) Back kick
Yoko-geri (yoh-koh geh-rhee) Side kick
Zen-kutsu-dachi (zen-koo-tsue dah-chee) Front stance

Index